*Color of Laughter -
Color of Tears*

by
Laurel A. Johnson
and
Stephen R. Sulik

© 2004 Stephen R. Sulik/Laurel A. Johnson
All rights reserved. Without limiting the rights under the copyright reserved above, no part of this publication may be reproduced, stored in or introduced into a retrieval system, or transmitted, in any form, or by any means (electronic, mechanical, photocopying, recording, or otherwise), without the prior written permission of both the copyright owner and the above publisher of this book. Brief passages may be quoted by reviewers to be printed in a newspaper, magazine, or online review site.

First Printing

Library Of Congress Control Number: 2004117197

Cover art by Kevin P. Grover
Cover photo design by Thomas A. Sulik

ISBN: 0-97624-714-3
PUBLISHED BY WINTERWOLF PUBLISHING
www.winterwolfpublishing.com
Westerville
Printed in the United States of America

811.6 J634c 2004
Johnson, Laurel A.
Color of laughter, color of tears

A Comment from the Authors

In times long past, poetry was the highest form of human expression. Today, that patina has been dulled somewhat, lost amidst the din of crashing vehicles and explosions on TV
and in the movies.

We long for solitude, quiet times to give our introspection voice. Noise feeds our ears without let up. Swirls of constant action and artificial light assault our eyes. We focus on a TV or movie screen and allow our dulled minds to vegetate. Our spirits and minds are weary, hoping to find respite.

As poets, we have chosen to put our peace or joy, our rage and sorrow into poems. Sometimes such words are all that keep us going for another minute, hour or day.

We dedicate this book to everyone we love.

May all your days

be filled
with tears of laughter.

Color of Laughter - Color of Tears

Table of Contents   Author

Foreword by Michael Corrigan

Prelude	Sulik
Universal Law	Sulik
Shifted	Johnson
Rescue Me	Sulik
Hopes and Prayers	Johnson
Revolving Door	Sulik
Path Finder	Sulik
Conflagration	Johnson
Hold Me Close	Sulik
Protection	Johnson
In Silent Reverie	Sulik
Remembering	Johnson
Smile for Me	Sulik
Before I Die	Johnson
Your Name is Special To Me	Sulik
The Transition	Johnson
Is There Someone There	Sulik
Charade	Johnson
Come Live With Me and Be My Inspiration	Sulik
My Silence	Johnson
The Rendezvous	Sulik
What Do You Have?	Johnson
The Watchman	Sulik
Hurting and Healing	Johnson
In Your Hands	Sulik
In Service	Sulik
Halfway Home	Johnson
Losing Myself for Hours	Sulik
Simple Miracles	Johnson
Work of Art	Sulik
Lost Friends	Johnson
Night Beat	Sulik
Burnout	Johnson

Color of Laughter - Color of Tears

Table of Contents **Author**

Outdoor Illusion	Sulik
I Search	Johnson
The Unlocked Door	Sulik
Bottom Line	Johnson
Mother	Sulik
Dad	Sulik
What Mother Did for Me	Johnson
Misty Sepia Memories	Johnson
Family Tree	Sulik
Wedding Song	Sulik
My One and True Valentine	Sulik
Sisters and Friends	Johnson
Forever Friends	Sulik
Miles Apart	Sulik
Color of Laughter, Color of Tears	Johnson
Giving Thanks	Sulik
The Rains Came	Sulik
The Chase	Sulik
Dreams	Johnson
Gift-Wrapped Package	Sulik
Fugue	Johnson
Committed Only to You	Sulik
I Wait	Johnson
Searching for Lost Love	Sulik
In Search of Paradise	Sulik
Soulmate	Sulik
Meeting	Johnson
The Knight and the Lady in White	Sulik
Life's Toll	Johnson
Outcast	Sulik
Markers	Johnson
Worst Case Scenario	Johnson
Benediction	Johnson
Closing Thoughts to Ponder	Unknown

FOREWORD

It's not often to find two poets in one edition unless they are part of a movement, like the romantics, Shelley and Keats. Stephen R. Sulik, a retired policeman, and Laurel Johnson, critic for the *Midwest Book Review*, have teamed up to produce a book of poetic meditations on life, love, and the inexorable passage of time. The book is **Color of Laughter-Color of Tears**, and represents the recent surge of interest in verse, from regional poetry festivals to self-published volumes. Who among these new poets will rank with world poets is the work of future critics, but the poems here attempt to capture the sounds of conversation, lines in the language of the common man.

Sulik's work can warmly celebrate a Christmas past but occasionally takes a dark turn as in "The Watchman" about a cop on a stake-out:

> For hours
> I remain still
> Alone on assignment
> inside cramped quarters
> not making a sound.

The lonely officer fills his hours with the memory of a lover's face. The feeling expressed is reminiscent of Dylan's "Tomorrow is a Long Time." Another poem captures the absurdity of the revolving prison doors and prisoners "awaiting freedom's call/to once again/ prey on the innocent."

Laurel Johnson's poems celebrate growth and relationships but also express rage at an abusive parent. In simple language, "Markers" is a bitter indictment of a gambler father forcing his wife into a life of slaving to pay his debts. One job entails slaughtering chickens. The poem is from the viewpoint of a bewildered child:

> I didn't understand it then,
> why she clutched the old cigar box
> to her chest the way she did.

Another poem called "Shifted" finds the child grown now, refusing to lament the death of a brutal father:

> He finally disappeared.
> All that remains is silence,
> blessed hollow spaces
> where his memory used to be.

There is a terror suggested by the "silences" of this poem. The anger recalls the intensity of Sylvia's Plath's poem, "Daddy."

Together, Sulik and Johnson represent two very different voices, simple, clear and resonant with feeling. Could there be a renaissance in regional poetry about to advance modern verse?

Michael Corrigan
2004

Editor's Note: Michael Corrigan teaches speech and English at Idaho State University, and is the author of **Confessions of a Shanty Irishman.** A collection of stories called **The Irish Connection and Other Stories** and a poetry chapbook titled **Irish Coffee** are scheduled for release by the fall of 2004.

Color of Laughter, Color of Tears

Prelude

When you have a quiet moment,
take off your shoes.
With the lights
turned low,
Recline in your
favorite chair
and find solace
within these pages.

Within our little book
are written impressions
of poetry
captured in simple form,
Conveying expressed feelings
of love,
Leaving their mark
on pages
that time
cannot erase.

— SRS —

Universal Law

Nature is art systematically
tuned, stable and balanced.
For every cause by man
there is an effect.
For every action
a reaction.
For every disaster
an opportunity to change.

When great minds and land
become corrupt and polluted,
Order in the world becomes
unbalanced, unstable and out of tune
with the One.
When the cancer spreads
Mother Nature retaliates,
Cleansing herself
of lies and disease.

Create constructively
in your endeavors,
To Know Who You Are
and Who You Are Not.
When people lose sight
of who they are −
They lose sight
of everything else.
Seek only the Truth
of Who You Really Are
and it will set you free.

Blessed are the Peacemakers.

The chosen are those
enlightened ones,
Who choose for themselves
above everything else,
To live their lives
for the One.

*All humanity and nature
are connected to One root,
Each of us
a Bright particle
of the Whole.*

May your spirit find true peace.

— SRS —

When we don't heed the Universal Law, disorder comes as a result. Our hearts harden. Spirits die, or come close to that. Peace eludes us as we lash out with what we know instead of trusting what we feel. Without peace, living in chaos, we are never free.

Shifted

There has been a shift
in my blunted sensibilities.
He finally disappeared.
All that remains is silence,
blessed hollow spaces
where his memory used to be.

Who cried the day he died?
Who said goodbye
or even cared that he was gone?
Who saw his essence fade
as he was laid to rest
or wished he was still with us
vibrant and alive?

Who will miss the best and worst of him:
the winning smile that flashed,
accompanied by laughter;
the rage that shattered flesh and bone;
the gentle voice so hypnotizing,
round with mellow baritone;
the fists he used as hammers to subdue
and bring to bear perverse delight;
the tears he shed regretfully
when everything he used as weapon
was exhausted for another day or week?

How can I speak of love or show remorse?
Pretend to miss him at his funeral?
And must I put a flower on his grave?
Hell no, I won't.
He's finally gone.

— LAJ —

Rescue Me

*I was born
wild
Free
to roam
Cities of glass
with concrete canyons*

*In the heart
of tinsel town
I survive
on my own
Without fear
of anyone
Desiring
to get close
to me*

*I belong
to no-one
Masquerading
in-between lies
Making exaggerated
excuses
Sharing my domain
with only those
like me*

*I have constant
urging visions
Of one day
fulfilling
my life's dream
Waking up
from a deep sleep
With aspiring ambition
Keeping a promise
to transform myself
From moth
to butterfly
Having no regrets
along the way
While searching
for the true me*

Color of Laughter, Color of Tears

Should you see me
w a n d e r i n g
The streets
in your city
And interested
in rescuing me
From the dangerous
g a u n t l e t
I play daily
Stop me –
before I fall
Hitting rock bottom
at a dead-end street

I am
w a s t i n g
away
Tired
of pretending
to be free
If given
the chance
I'll be forever
g r a t e f u l
to you
If you can help
tame
— wild me.

— SRS —

We all wish to be rescued, by time, circumstance, or an all powerful being who has our best interest at heart. Sometimes it happens, other times not, but it seems that humans always nurture hope.

Hopes and Prayers

When I was five and six and seven,
I prayed to be rescued from my father's rage.
That didn't happen,
at least not soon enough
to free my childhood of its fear.
Redemption came much later.

At eighteen, nineteen, twenty
I attempted resurrection and a failed escape
from work I knew
would take an awful toll,
destroy my soul and spirit over time.
I prevailed, but only after decades.

In my forties I lost Mother,
Grandma, Grandpa and at last my mind.
Life wasn't kind.
Hopes died, prayers went unanswered
as their life force slipped beyond my reach.
Eventually I muddled through.

And here I am today,
contemplating years of hopes and prayers.
I'm doing fine
in retrospect. Finding my own answers
brought a strength blind chance could never give.
I'm gearing up for the next decade.

—LAJ—

Revolving Door

Oh, windowless dungeon
surrounded by cold bars and boiler plates
From deep darkened corners
iron doors slam shut
echoing sounds behind escape-proof barriers.

Repulsive graffiti
curling and crawling from steel
Scratched by corroded minds
rebelling against justifiable cause
From thousands who visited
these nauseating cramped quarters-
a hell-hole
painted olive ugly.

Lives deteriorating on makeshift calendars
contributing nothing constructive
Playing endless mind games
on chess and checkered boards
Etched onto metal bunks
their squares covered by rust.

Locked away in a dank cell
nowhere to run
no place to hide
Awaiting freedom's call
to once again
Prey on the innocent
only to be-
Busted again.

One way in-
One way out-
Revolving door.

— SRS —

Path Finder

*Hungry and tired
a wandering traveler
Stood alone
in the howling wind
At the mouth
of a divided path –
One leading to the right;
the other to the left.*

*The traveler
was traumatized
By the sight
of a grotesque
Phantom fractured skull
staged in the dark sand
At the base
of a rotting sign
lettered in dried blood
On the less traveled path
to the right.*

*Shivering from cold fear
the traveler's attention
was diverted
When fleeing eyes
with lightning speed
darted across
To the more traveled path
to the left
Settling on a warm
enticing sign
Made of rainbow blinking
neon lights.*

*The traveler
with cupidity
tugging at his senses
Chose his destiny
deliberating not a second more
To follow
the flashy path
to the left.*

Color of Laughter, Color of Tears

The confident traveler
satisfied with his
split-second decision
Took a headlong side-step
to his left
Beginning his journey
on his chosen path.

A lightning bolt struck
as the traveler's
Conscience
gave warning
Hinting
at imminent peril ahead
For him to retreat
and follow the path
to the right.

The traveler's
obstinate determination
attempted to erase doubt
Unwilling to submit
to any cognitive suggestion.

The traveler struggled
with his conscience
losing in the end
when sound perseverance prevailed
The traveler
was overruled
against his present course
by a Higher Enlightenment.

*The traveler
reconsidered
without further argument
Before starting
on his pilgrimage
on the right path
The traveler's
obscured observation
cleared
When further inspection
of the signs
revealed
they had been –
Switched.
—SRS—-*

Conflagration

Cold eyed and empty hearted,
you left your harsh edged world behind
and entered mine in search of sanctuary.
What you found was love,
a one-man-woman in disguise
as walking wounded.

Love lit a match.
We couldn't quite believe the outcome.

Your first kiss said it all,
as if your thoughts were cast in stone.
Despair. Starvation. Shattered hopes.
Pent up tenderness that tore your heart
and quivered at my mouth
with such a poignant hunger
that it left me wildly weeping
with a sudden understanding in its wake.

I was the timid fluttering flame,
and you the wind that fanned the fire
from fading light 'til morning sun.
The conflagration almost burnt us both to ash.
Out of fear and ignorance,
I wondered if we could survive
a long association. You laughed,
"Somehow I bet we manage to adapt."

—LAJ—

Hold Me Close

Sometimes I feel
 as though I've lost
  my anchor

        Drifting far out
         to sea
          in my tiny boat

                Furthering the distance
                between you and me
                Hoping not to sink
                 and drown
                - never to return.

       Hearing comforting
        reassuring words
         from your
       Soft effeminate voice
        brings me back to reality

Anchoring me
  firmly in place
   again
    - by your side.

— SRS —

Protection

I learned the meaning of protection early.
470J was the number that would call up safety
because familiar voices always answered.
Grandma and Grandpa lived there
at the other end of the phone line.

And late at night when our old house was scary,
with crying behind that awful bedroom door
or stumbling shadows lurking near my bed,
if I could make it to the phone beside Mom's rocker
the angry shadow would be sure to disappear.

Some nights I huddled in the rocker in Mom's sweater
and strained to see the big tree on our parking.
A tall and broad man often stood there,
a sleepy silent guardian of his daughter
and her children, just in case he might be needed.

Later there were uncles, and finally a husband,
all decent men who used their strengths to nurture,
not abuse or keep a female beaten down or frightened.
These were the quiet unassuming hallmarks who demonstrated
by example what a man should be.

—LAJ—

In Silent Reverie

Through my eyes
I have witnessed
Incredible beauty
in this world
Perfection
in all
God's glory
From the simplest
of plants
to the most
magnificent beasts
All things
shouting Love
from the One
Who created and made
it all possible for us
to enjoy.

My only wish in life
during these times
I am most enthralled
and inspired by such
fascinating beauty
Is to be able to share
these simple
precious moments
with no one else
- but you.

— SRS —

Love is precious in all its forms. From that first fiery thrall of knowing who we want, to the last tear shed in parting, love - or the longing for it - is the finest thread of which our reveries are spun. More accomplished poets than I will ever be have woven from that thread, but the beauty of poetry is that everyone can speak from the heart.

Remembering

    I watch his hands, remembering
    how powerful they used to be,
        how warm
      those work rough palms,
        how soft
  the touch of those long fingers
    as they brushed my cheek
    or wrapped around my arms.

    I look into his eyes, remembering
    the brown eyed handsome man
        he was
      when we first met,
  how sweet he seemed the day
       those eyes
quite boldly met and held my stare
  with humor dancing in them.

    I kiss his mouth, remembering
  the subtle magic he could work,
        the joy
  when it turned up into a smile,
the shape and velvet texture of it,
      the taste
  that was not like any other
    for me then or now.

    I give a hug, remembering
  the days when he was taller,
      the times
that wondrous frame was stronger
  with the urgency of youth,
      the love
  that passed between us
  in our heated moments.

*Sometimes I cry, remembering
the years when both of us
were younger,
stronger, passionately longing for
each other in the dark,
or light.
But other times I smile,
remembering.*

— LAJ —

Smile for Me

If I could
say something
To wipe away
your tears
To comfort
your tired
weary spirit
To help ease
the pain
and heal
your wound
You carry deep
within your heart

I would whisper
these simple words
in your ear –

I carry a torch
for no other
but you
Your hurt
is my hurt
I cannot continue on
until the sadness
Disappears from your
lovely face
I realize more than ever
with each passing day
You are my life
I have no purpose
without you
My wish is to see again
– your sweet smile.

— SRS —

Laurel A. Johnson/Stephen R. Sulik

Before I Die

I was thinking just the other day
that before I die
I'd like to see the ocean.
Breakers crashing on a rocky shore
would take my spirit to another place
and bring the smile back to my face
for just a little while, perhaps.
If I could only be there
in the fresh salt air
and feel the mists of ages on my skin,
I might survive a decade longer,
feel much stronger in my waning years,
shed fewer tears of loss and sorrow.
Surely the ocean's power
is a gift that every poet-writer
ought to give herself before she dies.

I'd like to have my smile back,
like it was in younger days, with teeth
of purest ivory white,
taking in both friend and stranger
until their grin is matching mine
and life is fine and pure because they see
the beauty in me, waiting to burst free
from homely-looking bonds.

And I'd like to make love one more time.
Despite my age, is that too much to ask
of an all powerful Creator,
a reprise of purest carnal pleasure
as he takes one final precious measure
of the space and span my spirit reaches
when it's taken there by tenderness?

I must confess to wanting more than God intends to give.
What can I expect? He'll let me live
to a ripe old age without you,
the ocean, or my smile.

—LAJ—

Your Name Is Special To Me

I like to say your name
whenever we are together -
In private comforting arms at home
or at family gatherings in the park
or upon a public street with friends.

Your name is echo soft
that rises and lingers above the rafters,
Forever meaning a fond hello
but never once
- meaning a sad farewell.

Your name rings high in the sky
reminding me of church bells
Lifting my spirit and inspiring me
to new soaring heights
and keeping my courage strong.

I repeat your name in my sleep -
it makes me feel secure all night
Knowing when the sun breaks early dawn
shining through cottony clouds
on a gray day
You are there beside me
to make me smile bright with cheer
when I awake.

Your name
is the magic melody in my life
that keeps me going -
Making each new day glow
with love we share within our hearts
Holding each other close
-even when we are apart.

—SRS—

The Transition

Somewhere between the hurdy gurdy
and the sturm und drang, something changed.
I crashed, or had a change of opinion.
Old goals and aspirations lost importance,
and I began to search beneath my superficial surface
for a genuine persona, something real
that I could use as anchor to ride out life's storms.
I'd always been a chameleon,
changing personalities and colors to appease,
never saying what I really thought, not
revealing my true feelings to the world.
But finally I stopped pretending
to be something that I'm not. I learned a lot.
No longer the invariably smiling sap
and everyone's best friend, best nurse,
best sister, granddaughter, wife or child,
I settled into a rather wild transition.
Nobody liked the change much, especially me,
but now I'm free to be myself
despite a million bone deep imperfections.
It's been a great relief.

—LAJ—

Is There Someone There

*Is there someone there
who will stay and listen
to my song.*

*Is there someone there
who can take the time
to understand
what I have to say.*

*Is there someone there
who I can love forever
and a day
And I, too,
be loved
by someone there.*

*Is there someone there
who cares to know
- what love is.*

— SRS —

Rarely is love pure and untainted by our past. We drag with us the baggage that we've carried from forgotten childhood happenings. Entire lifetimes of loving can be lost, or may be pale shadows of potential joy in our need to protect ourselves.

Charade

There was a time you didn't understand
the workings of my heart.
You turned a cold and disapproving face
on everything I did.
At least that's how it seemed to me
back then when we were young.
I didn't understand the fear you felt
when I was out of sight,
or realize the pain that came of thinking
you might lose me to another, better man.
That hard and disapproving face
you turned on me,
your vicious cutting words,
were a disguise you used
in hopes I'd never get the upper hand
and kill your spirit with rejection.
In other words, you hurt me first
and best, hoping you might win.
But I caught on to your charade.
I loved you 'til you cried,
and kept on loving.
I almost died
from needing you to love me back
as hard and strong as I loved you.
You came around,
not in our younger days
when both of us might reap the benefit
of trusting passion,
but soon enough that we could keep
those promises we made in front of God
so long ago.

— LAJ —

Come Live With Me and Be My Inspiration

*Come –
live with me*

*On a deserted
sandy beach
Near a shiny
blue sea*

*Where time
is forgotten*

*And love
remembered.*

*Come
live with me*

*Where the air
is fresh
and pure*

*The sky
crystal clear.*

*Come
listen
to the birds*

*Serenading across
calm waters.*

*Come
be my inspiration
and live in my love.*

— SRS —

My Silence

I'd rather that my failing heart
should flutter in a silent cage
or cease pulsating altogether
than to ever hurt you.
Your life, and my presence in it,
has always seemed a gift to me.

Today I ponder retrospectively
the years we've shared.
My words are woefully inadequate,
nor can you fully understand the feelings
that remain unspoken.
Love is like a pain in me.

I learned to hide my thoughts in childhood,
and cover them with sunny smiles
regardless of the sorrows I might feel.
You, on the other hand, spoke out
with rage or laughter,
whatever you were feeling at the time.

You expressed desire or disapproval.
I alternately swooned or cringed
inside my mind in mostly silence.
You couldn't always read my mind
as I expected you to do,
which left me floundering for words.

My words have always flowed on paper,
not in the air between us.
Misunderstandings came as a result,
each and every one my fault
and mine alone. I don't communicate,
except in written words.

Every love psalm, each tender story
centered around you. My feelings,
so inexpressible in spoken words,
took wings whenever I could find the strength
to write them down. I struggled,
afraid my words would fall on empty space.

Color of Laughter, Color of Tears

Often my meanings were obtuse,
disguised in metaphor or simile.
And if you questioned me
I stammered indistinct replies
that left you guessing, wishing
I could just spit out my thoughts in simple words.

OK, here goes, I'll try.
But you will have to read the words
I still can't say aloud.
I need you more than air or water.
I've always loved you more than life or breath.
Your energy and strength are nourishment to me.

I've said it all before in every book,
each poem written through the years.
I'm worthless without you, so helpless
that I barely can survive when you're not with me.
I'm hoping you believe and understand,
forgive, accept, embrace my silence.

—LAJ—

The Rendezvous

*The only sounds heard
come from a rocking boat's
creaking wood planks
anchored off the mainland*

*Surrounded by serene
blue waters and
grandeur colored skies
of the splendid night ahead*

*An amusing smile
creases my weathered face
bringing pleasure
to dancing eyes.*

*Leaning back
in tranquility
I watch
the cool September breeze
caress your sleek golden hair*

*Your irresistible
captivating eyes
Conquer mine
leaving me breathless
with warm yearning reflections
of you
Keeping me company
on our sensual rendezvous
at twilight*

*Living a sentimental journey
to reminisce for eternity
Before returning
to shore
- at dawn's early light.*

— SRS —

Whether fulfilled or unrequited, love is a part of life. Time, distance, past, present and future blend, revealing themselves in hidden moments as a dream, wish, or unexpected thought.

What Do You Have?

I have my music –
tough tender melodies
that take me through the night
alone and weeping.
What do you have?

I have my memories –
half forgotten pangs
that wake me trembling
from a haunted sleep.
What do you have?

I have my brass and copper treasures
sitting all around the house
to catch the glow of candle light.
And you?
What gets you through and salves the pain?

Why do I weep and tremble?
I'm not sure,
unless the two of us were ancient lovers
trapped in a desire so strong
the feel of you still lingers
as a long forgotten memory.
That must be it.

In ages past we must have shared a love
that burned too hot and fast.
The power of it must have nearly killed us both.
In ages past we surely knew a finer time
than what we struggle through today.
I found a way to soothe myself
and make it through.
But what of you?

-- LAJ -

The Watchman

For hours
I remain still
Alone on assignment
inside cramped quarters
Not making a sound
to give my position away.

Wide trained eyes
spy the full moon
appearing over the horizon
While a bone-chilling freeze
sweeps across
death valley.

Preying on shadows
I remain on alert
for the enemy
Under stars
that sparkle
miles away from home
Separating me
from being with you.

As the night
wears on
My mind shifts
and begins d r i f t i n g
B e c o m i n g o c c u p i e d
f i l l i n g d a r k l o n e l y
e m p t y s p a c e s
W i t h w a r m i m a g e s
of your radiant face
D r e a m i n g
desirable thoughts
of me
Surrendering
- only to you.

— SRS —

We are our memories, whether they live at the conscious or unconscious level. I can't help but wonder sometimes how many spirits wither because we don't comprehend our behavior well enough to help others understand. We all need help along the way. Some of us are blessed enough to get exactly the help we need.

Hurting and Healing

Pain came calling in the dark of night,
leaving a child afraid and drained of hope,
marked indelibly by violence.

Years passed.
Memories of those awful nights
lay buried in a grownup mind,
but then returned to haunt me
at the first touch of your hand
on fear numbed skin.

I shrank beneath that touch,
relived the past,
remembered everything
that once brought horror
to a fearful child.
You backed away.

Despite hot blood and youth
you wisely let that fear subside,
and over time your touch
began to speak to me of love,
not pain or childish panic.
Yes, you were wise.

And then, beneath the pine,
on fragrant needle bed,
you laid to rest the coldness
in a child's once frightened heart.
You wrapped yourself around me
underneath the stars.

I knew safety for the first time
and learned that love could be,
not so much pain,
but purest pleasure, sweet delight.
Laughter came of it
and freedom from despair.

— LAJ —

In Your Hands

*You have given me
a chance to be free
as I wish to be*

*You parted
mighty waters
Cleared darkened
clouds
Opened the sky
allowing the sun
to etch across
the galaxy*

*Traveling by air
I feel a spirit
Protecting me
wherever I venture*

*On land
a guiding light
Shows me
the way*

*At sea
sensing Your presence
keeps me afloat*

*Trusting my life
is secured
While in Your hands.*

— SRS —

In Service
10-8
On Patrol

   My partner was stricken once --
knocked down to the ground
  and out cold --
Winded,
  he regained his strength
Managing to return
  to the beat he loved --
In Service
  10-8
    On Patrol.

My partner was wounded again
  falling harder than before --
Hastening to regain control
  he was soon on his feet
    and back to his favorite beat --
In Service
  10-8
    On Patrol.

My partner was overwhelmed
  a third time
Not knowing for sure
  if he would ever recover
    and return --
Staggering,
  he climbed to his feet
Standing tall --
In Service
  10-8
    On Patrol.

My partner's day
  of rest arrived
I will miss him --

*No more suffering pain
would he endure
 I know he's back
    on his feet though
 Feeling revived
and walking tall
 on his new beloved beat
In Service
  10-8
    Patrolling the Gates
         of Heaven.*

—SRS—-

Halfway Home

We lived two blocks from school when I was five.
Ours was a safe town then, no surprises,
only a railroad bum from time to time
in search of food or water between trains.
Even the Kindergarten kids like me
walked to school and back
no matter what the weather.

Mom always said, "Stick to the sidewalk,
don't walk in the alley."

Despite my tender age I knew
that was one of life's important lessons.
She was saying, stay with the familiar,
the sidewalk leads you straight to our front door.
When winter came she took my mittened hand
and walked with me to school.
Every step of the way she demonstrated
what to do in case of blizzard.
I can hear her voice today, still feel her hand.

"Feel that little groove between the sidewalk
and the grass? Put one foot there
and keep it there, just slide that foot along,
one foot in the groove, the other on the sidewalk."

We passed two blocks together holding hands,
hobbling stiff legged, dragging one foot
just off the sidewalk's edge.

She said, "In case of blizzard, don't be scared.
Just walk along the edge the way we did today.
I'll come and meet you.
Before you're halfway home we'll run across each other."

It happened just the way she said.
Miss Kruse helped me cross the street
and find the sidewalk, then that tell-tale groove.

Laurel A. Johnson/Stephen R. Sulik

I slid my foot the way Mom said,
lost in that white world of snow and howling wind.
And halfway home I heard her call my name
above the wind that tried to snatch her voice away.
I collided with her so familiar softness halfway home.
Just one of my child's storehouse of memories,
reminding me that today I'm halfway home.
It's warm where Mother is, and safe.
I know she's watching for me.

—LAJ—

Losing Myself for Hours

When I'm near
fatal exhaustion
There's a place
I often visit
Far up
in the luxurious
green hills
I venture
away from it all

Losing myself
in my sacred site
I sit for hours
in a meditative trance
Becoming a part
of the silence
surrounding me

With each
fleeting moment
that passes
I regain strength
peace of mind
and total confidence
To return
to the intolerant world
- below.

— SRS —

Simple Miracles

Mother always told me I was born too late
by at least a hundred years.
Now that she's gone,
and I'm the age that she was
when she said it,
I've had to face it: She was right.

Where is the utter quiet
humans knew before machines
began to belch their poison
into once pure air?
I want only bird songs
or a whispering of wind,
thunder and the sound of rain
to break my silences.

Where is the isolation
of the prairies after sunrise
as tall grass begins to whisper
subtle morning greetings?
I long for solitude,
time for gathering my thoughts
in blessed separating space
untouched by others.

Mother, you were right.
Whatever modern life has stolen
from me, here and now,
I want it back.
Where are the simple miracles
I might have known
a hundred years ago or more?

—LAJ –

Work of Art

*A weaver
intertwines
by hand
a domain*

*Uniting
Two different worlds
into one*

*Fulfilling
a promise
To serve
and protect
Without bias.*

*The closer
he spins
his thread
The stronger
the bond*

*Flourishing
roots
Bearing
fruit
Withstanding
outside forces
that neither
Wind
Cold
nor Drought
can destroy
The weaver's
- quintessence.*

— SRS —

Lost Friends

No matter what my situation,
right or wrong, she took me in.
Her love was not saved up for rainy days.
She loved the ones she loved without condition,
regardless whether they returned in kind.
When we first met, co-workers warned,
"Watch out! She'll eat you up alive!"
I found the opposite was true that day
and every day thereafter.
Everything about her was a gift from that day forth.
She loved fried chicken, sexy romance novels,
scented candles, wine and cheese.
And she took great pride in everything I did.
I didn't dare attend her funeral,
convinced myself I'd honored her in life.
I hope I did, at least.

To take her place an angel came
from out of cyberspace.
Oh, how I loved that laughing angel!
The course of life for her had not been smooth.
Somehow she made the most of every trial
and laughed about rough patches with her friends.
She gave her all in everything,
sacrificed to help her children,
spread affection over everyone she knew.
She was well read, intelligent,
could talk with anyone on any subject,
yet had the common touch and ribald humor.
The day she died was almost more than I could bear.
She lived so far away and hid her illness from me
at the end. She was my friend,
my precious angel. How I miss her.

—LAJ—

Night Beat

I travel quiescent
deserted streets
From one end
of town
to the other.

Back and forth
on my beat
I drive,
Making countless
loops
with nothing astir.

I hear the same
barking dogs
and alley cats
From the night before
making their synchronized
presence known
As I cruise by
dirty darkened windows
of silent shadowy buildings.

Hour
after monotonous hour
slips away.

A train whistles in the distance -
Soon
the guilty sandman
is caught sneaking around
my beat again,
Taking his toll
on innocent me.

In the face of daylight
he convinces me
To let him go.

Now off duty
I chase him
over the rainbow,
Only to find him
already in bed
When I get home.

—SRS –

Those who have a calling to "protect and serve" so often go down in flames. And when they do, they occasionally go beyond burnout, past reclamation. Those who fall are frequently the bright, shining, idealistic ones. In youth, anything is possible, but as we age we sometimes learn sad lessons. Since time began, situations stay the same. Only the faces change.

Burnout

Life has become an endless repetition
of the same people
saying the same endless things
while wearing different faces.

How did it come down to this?

Where is the milk of human kindness
that used to run so strong
through my veins and heart?

How did I lose
that idealistic young girl I was
not that many years ago?

Why did the passion leave me,
that desire to dispense comfort
and save the world from suffering?

And why am I exhausted
all the time, through every season?
Does anybody know the reason?

Am I in burnout?
Gone beyond that to despair
from failing in my quest
to make a difference?

Somebody help me.
I've fallen and I can't get up.

—LAJ -

Outdoor Illusion

*Standing at a distance
I could hear
My favorite song
being played,
A spectacular sound
echoing through
the recesses of my mind.
Within me
the vibrations erupt
As I approach
the outdoor concert
in the park's gazebo.*

*The quartet consisted
of well-tailored musicians
Playing a romantic ballad
with a stimulating
rhythmic beat.
I hope some day
to compose
An overture
of my own
And perform in front
of a live audience.*

*When I arrive
at the gazebo,
My favorite song fades and
Is lost somewhere
deep within my consciousness.
I expect the band
will receive
A standing ovation
for their musical talents.
As I glance around
no-one is gathered
here today
And the gazebo
is vacant.*

*But it does not matter
- I cannot hear.*

— SRS —

I Search

Is it genetic imprints,
half-buried memories,
or imagination that inspires this déjà vu?
A place and time, a person haunts me.

Crisp night air envelopes strong bare legs.
Frozen waist high grass scratches as I walk.
An owl whoooos mournfully in the distance
and behind me a coyote yips from hiding.
I'm alone, breathless with dread,
searching for safe haven in the dark.
Night stars and low-slung moon
shine bright white against a black infinity.
Night scents are strong,
each element inhabiting the air distinct,
alive and pleasing to my nose.
I sniff the wind for hints of burning wood
or roasting meat. My stomach growls
its protest as saliva forms in answer
to the thought of food.
The covering I wear is skin and fur.
It warms my head and upper body
as I search for warmth and shelter.
The night seems endless,
that ancient prairie lonesome but familiar
to this spectre from another place and time.

—LAJ—

The Unlocked Door

*In front
of this locked door
Stands a person
we all know,
Ready to respond
to an inner
secret urge
To challenge
the outside world
On the other side.*

*Yearning
for an opportunity
to try a magic key
To unlock
a hidden talent
Different from
any other.*

*Striving to play
the game
of survival
Developing
an instinct
To succeed
in life.*

*Matured
to accept
misfortunes
Realizing
other chances
Should the first
key fail.*

— SRS —

Bottom Line

Money and the getting of it
has never been my bottom line.
Money doesn't feed my spirit
or keep me warm at night
with body heat.

Yes, I have to pay my bills but...
I prefer love over money,
friendship over wealth,
and family over dollar signs.
That's how I am.

What do I value more than money?

Slow dancing.
Lost in the music and mood,
nothing or no one else exists
around me at the time
except the arms that hold me
and the man I'm held by.

Writing.
Making the words come alive
as only I can do
to suit myself, not others,
loving the characters and places
into vibrant life on paper.

Making love.
Knowing the love maker accepts me
exactly as I am
with all my weaknesses and strengths,
despite the glaring fact
that I'm no raving beauty.

That's enough to make my point.
Money has never been my bottom line.
It pays the bills, that's all,
and buys the food we eat,
the clothes we wear.
It cannot, does not, produce love.

— LAJ —

Mother

Mother dear –

*Words alone
cannot express
the Love
and gratitude*

*We cherish for having
such a special person
as you.*

*Let trumpets blare
in heaven and
angels rejoice on high*

*So all the world
will hear*

*There is
no other
- like our mother.*

— SRS —

Dad

*The admiration
and respect
I have
for you, Dad,
is found deep
within my heart.*

*Seeing the courage
you possess
As you struggle
with life's obstacles
day after day
Has made me strong
to carry on
with my own load.*

*There are times
when I have seen you
With pain
and sorrow
Causing you
to stumble and fall.*

*But because
of the person
you are inside
Were able to rise up
against adversity,
Brush yourself off
to stand tall
once again,
Pressing forward
to hurdle wall
after wall.*

*I am proud
and honored
To have you
- as my father.*

— SRS —

What Mother Did for Me

My mother cleaned chickens for a living,
back when Dad left her with four children
to feed, support, and love without his help,
and a stack of unpaid bills to pay
while he drank and danced the light fantastic
with one in an endless line of other women.

That was in the days before child support,
welfare or food stamps came along.

Relatives or good Christian folk
did what they could to help a needy woman,
and her ragamuffin children.
It was never enough though,
so Mom cleaned chickens. An awful job.

The stench of chicken entrails never left me,
her oldest child who knew what cleaning chickens meant.
The fading memories of decades
will not banish what I saw and smelled
My mother's face, fire engine red and sweating
in the Kansas summer heat, the smell of blood and guts
and chicken feathers scalded in hot water
live on to haunt me along with Mother's tears.

Cleaning chickens was not on the path
she would have chosen for herself in better times.
But still, she did it.
Hundreds of squawking chickens died
beneath her butcher knife while Mother shed hot tears
of sorrow and frustration,
cleaning chickens for a living so her kids could eat.

— LAJ —

Misty Sepia Memories

*Grandma came to me in dreams last night
the way she always does,
obscure, just out of reach.
She gives me messages that I can't hear,
or if I hear them clearly,
the fuller meaning must escape me.
She's always miles and miles away at first.
I have to take a crowded plane to reach her,
or ride in battered ancient Chevys
with her long dead brothers.
The house she lives in, once we reach it,
is no place I have ever been before.
In other dreams she lives in shadowed places,
empty rooms that hold her essence
or the well-remembered scent of her –
vanilla in her cookies or the fragrance
of her fresh-baked bulgur bread.
I search for her through misty sepia memories,
back through time, frustrated at her absence.
Despite my frequent dreams of her,
I rarely find the woman who was Grandma,
just a figment wrapped within a cryptic message
I can't begin to translate.*

— LAJ —

Family Tree

*Seeds
sown together*

*Nurtured
by Love
and tender care
while growing*

*Reproducing life
that blossoms
and branches
outward*

*Forming
new seeds
and new beginnings.*

— SRS —

Wedding Song

I wish you both
all the fulfillment
Love can bring,
Joy to make
your hearts gladden,
Sadness to bring
you closer together.
Now that you
are united as one,
I hope you will strive
to reach any star
you desire,
Encouraging one another
in accomplishing your goals.

Even though strife
and storms
may come your way,
Always remember
they will pass
and sunshine
Shall come again.

Together
you will travel
along your chosen path
Discovering many
spectrums of the
Rainbow called life.

May all your feelings
be looked upon
with thankful hearts,
For you both
will experience
all the wonders
and variety
The Master
created for you.

— SRS —

Laurel A. Johnson/Stephen R. Sulik

My One and True Valentine

If I should say a thousand thanks
  I know in my being
They would not be sufficient words
  for all the joy you have brought into my life.

They could not begin
  to tell you how much
Your companionship has meant to me
  and all it has contributed
    to keep my heart content.

How happy you have made me
  through all the years we've been together
With your patience and understanding smile
  and how the very thought of you -
    has made my life worthwhile.

My only sad moments
  are those when you are away
Because your presence means so much
  to help me face each new day.

And that is why a thousand thanks
  however sweet and true
Would never be enough
  to give my gratitude to you -
My lifeline
   - my Valentine.

— SRS —

Sisters and Friends

*You're my friend and my sister,
bound to me by kinship of the heart
and spirit.*

*You've hugged me close in bad times,
shared my wings in good.
We've crawled and flown together,
you and I.*

*And what a blessed gift it is,
to know that you're my friend and ally,
my sister.*

— LAJ —

Forever Friends

*Thank you
for being my
close friend,
Allowing me
into your day,
For telling me
things I've never
known about before,
For taking me places
I've only dreamed
of being.
You have shared
with me
Your valuable time
and private world,
For which I
am grateful.
I shall
always cherish
and honor
our true friendship.*

— SRS —

Miles Apart

Living
in different parts
of the country
Miles
cannot separate
The chance
for us
to accomplish
A genuine goal
together.

Each begins
a new chapter
of adventure,
Undertaking the task
to complete
a unique idea.

Though creative minds
sometimes differ,
Each works
with pride
as a team,
Allowing
the other room
to explore
Mysteries
of the universe
without criticism.

Proving
by believing in
and sharing experiences
Contributes
to benefiting
the overall
achievement.

— SRS —

Laurel A. Johnson/Stephen R. Sulik

Color of Laughter, Color of Tears

We live far apart now,
but nothing
has changed between us.
I still love you.

I can still see your face,
the smile in your eyes
that gladdened me
each time we met.

I remember the hugs,
the tears we shed together,
the laughter and the secrets
shared with no one else.

If friendship had a name,
if tears and laughter had a color,
it would be yours, my friend.

— LAJ —

Giving Thanks

Thanksgiving is a day of prayer
for everyone near and far to share
In giving thanks to God above
for providing us many things to love.

We should give thanks
for this great land
Where everyone
lends a helping hand
To all his neighbors,
brothers and sisters
In bringing to them
hope and cheer.

We should give thanks
that we are safe
From strife and worries
and bitter hate
While those who are engaged in war
shall know world peace -
forever more.

We should give thanks for our freedom
for the food we eat, the water we drink
For our joys and our health
for vastly riches or humble wealth.

We should give thanks every single day
not only when Thanksgiving day
comes our way
But every minute of the hour
give prayers and thanks
- to our Great Power.

— SRS —

Laurel A. Johnson/Stephen R. Sulik

The Rains Came

The rains came
without a warning

Out in the field
with no place to go

Running somewhere
I do not know.

The rains came
bringing a misty curtain
of droplets
of warm water,

Rinsing me clean
in the summer
scented shower,

Refreshing my heart
and soul

When the rains came.

— SRS —

The Chase

Cloud formations
in the distant sky
Funny shapes
and sizes
floating by.

In the mighty
heavens above
I watch as you
flee from me –
Soaring
on the wings
of an angel
In the late
afternoon
summer breeze.

Swift
as the wind
you run
Laughing
with me
in close pursuit —
As if there was
no tomorrow.

Setting an
unbreakable pace
Through a wide open
obstacle course —
I dream
of catching you
soon —
Before you leave
me far behind —
With a pack of yipping coyotes
— at the end of the day.

— SRS —

Dreams

When did the dreams end?
I can't remember.
I used to do my best work
in dreams.

Inspirations, validations,
sweet encouragements
used to come in dreams
at night.

I do know that loss ended them
and only hope
will bring them back
to life.

Let go of loss and reach for hope
is their advice.
I'm not sure I can
just yet.

— LAJ —

Gift-Wrapped Package

Beneath
the decorative scent
of the balsam tree
Was a gift-wrapped package
on Christmas Eve.

Its contents disguised
with ribbons and bows
awaited
Christmas Day.

As a child
waiting with
anxious anticipation
For the signal
from watchful parents,
The final few seconds
of the countdown
to begin the festivities
Always seemed
the longest.

Treasuring those
special moments
Of those early years
now brings a quiet tear
Or two
to my eyes.

Wishing more
than ever
to return
To those wonderful
childhood feelings,
To once again
experience
innocent times

When true Love
was a gift-wrapped
package
under the balsam tree
Labeled - 'Fragile'
Handle with Care
- on Christmas Eve.

— SRS —

Fugue

I stare at the pictures,
lost in a trance,
focusing on long lost yesterdays.

There's me,
smiling that sunny way
I used to
when the Brownie box camera came out.
Easter Sunday, all decked out
in finery my mother made by hand,
Shirley Temple curls gleaming
in the morning sun.
God, I was pretty then,
in my innocence and childish pride,
still waiting for the Easter Bunny.

Me again,
wearing a false white beard
and a Santa hat cocked sideways,
stuffed into a padded Santa suit
and boots,
on my way to playing Santa
for Aunt Lois's sorority.
I barely remember it.

And me,
a chubby toddler.
No wonder everybody loved me then!
I was so beautiful, so pure,
with spun gold hair,
smiling sweetly with my little arms
reaching to be held
by someone just off camera.

Somewhere in me, that child lives,
still pure and innocent,
expectant of the best,
still believing love is just
a reach away.

— LAJ —

Committed Only To You

Suspended in
animation
I stand
entranced
in front of you
Your hungry
ravishing eyes
Penetrate mine
as I listen
To the call
of the wild
within me

Loving thoughts
of being
Committed
to you
Linger in my mind
mid-flight
Together we paint the skies
in shades of autumn leaves
Singing glorious hymns
at heaven's gate
From this day
to eternity

I remain
fascinated
By your dazzling
inner beauty
Hypnotized
while adoring
The stunning contours
of your wholesome
features

The spontaneous passion
I feel towards you
Is true
innocent and pure
Longing to hold
you forever close
To hear
the cadence
Of our attuning hearts
— melting together.

— SRS —

I Wait

I've had my times
but nothing will be whole until I find you.
I missed you in the Highlands.
You died young.
Through bogs and moors I searched,
alone and lonely.
I fought the winds
that howled across an ancient plain,
found fleeting passion in the waving grasses
but he wasn't you.
I scanned petroglyphs in winter,
shivering while searching for your sign
and hoping you'd be mine again.
Sometimes I can feel you in the night.
I wait for light and pray
to find your essence on me somewhere.
My imagination fools me,
or maybe it's my pounding heart
and vessels throbbing out your name.
Nothing is the same without you here
and so I wait.

— LAJ —

Searching for Lost Love

In the silence of night
I lay awake
Longing for the love
we once shared
in history past.

Searching the darkness
of my empty room
I vision you
appearing someday
before me
To take away forever
the tears
and giving purpose
to my life.

During our brief encounter
centuries ago
We loved a lifetime
when our lives crossed
in the Highlands.

Upon returning
from battle
for freedom
I searched all the land
for you my love
But,
you were nowhere
to be found.

Laurel A. Johnson/Stephen R. Sulik

*Ever since that day
in time
There has been
for me
No other –
but you.
In my quest
I scour the earth
each time
my spirit returns
In hopes
of finding and
holding you close
once again against
my pulsating heart
Never again –
to leave your side.*

— SRS —

In Search of Paradise

A lighthouse kindles
a deserted beach
with a faint glow

In the milky twilight
we journey along
our memory lane

Splashing warm waters
at the ocean's edge
massage our feet

In the sea breeze
your rose perfume
permeates my nose

I feel a sudden rush
of quivering adrenaline
Electrifying every nerve fiber
in my body

I give you a side-glance wink,
smile and steal a quick kiss
from your voluptuous honey lips

I feel stimulated
when my pulsating blood quickens
Streaking through subway veins
faster than the speed of light
reaching a rocky mountain high

Grasping hands
we laugh and sprint towards
the transcendental horizon

Disappearing
— in Shangri La.

— SRS —

Laurel A. Johnson/Stephen R. Sulik

Soulmate

*From behind
an oak tree
I watch
in silence
As the songbirds
serenade you
from above*

*In my daily ritual
I follow close behind
To keep you
from harms way
As you stroll alone
through the foothills
Filled with bluebonnets
and Indian paintbrush*

*Hope and faith
entered my life
The first time
I saw your face
In the field
of dreams*

*My bashful heart
echoes a sad tune
of loneliness
For the right moment
to reach out
Making my presence known
to meet you
Connecting us
to the web of life*

*As if having
mental telepathy
You turn around
with grace
Holding out your hand
you catch me off guard
causing me to blush*

Color of Laughter, Color of Tears

Your rhinestone eyes
capture mine
Lighting up my life
giving me sustenance
As I place
my hand
in yours
While walking
we bond together
Making a pledge
of allegiance
To our newfound
friendship
To honor
nurture and trust
One another
- until the end of time.

— SRS —

Meeting

My world is soft-edged,
alive with pastel colors,
hopeful and secure.
I finally found peace
after many years of struggle.

You stumbled onto me -
world-weary, drained -
in search of fuel or manna
to allay a raging hunger
that had gone beyond controlling.

Blinded by the fullness,
you groped your way along
the bright perimeters
you sensed but could not see.
You searched for me
until the softness drew you in.

The sorrow carried with you
spoke of dark despairs
beyond my world's imagination.
I peeled each layer gently back
until the shrinking soul of you shone through.

What can we do,
now that our lives have blended?
Which impish muse or smiling God
ordained this meeting?
The answer to that question is a mystery.

— LAJ —

The Knight and the Lady in White

Looking up
into the heavens
We sit
among the daisies
and lilies of the field
Dreaming of
royal enchanted castles
in the air

A gentle breeze
brushes wisps
Of your hair
over your
Tanned shoulders

The look of love
is in my eyes
Wishing to be stranded
on a deserted island
with no one but you

As you tease
your hair
I pick a flower
to play
She loves me
She loves me not
Hoping the last petal
will trap me
In your love
forever

I lean over
to whisper in your ear
You are my
Lady of Shalott
I want to be
your loyal
Red-cross knight –
Sir Lancelot
of Camelot

Laurel A. Johnson/Stephen R. Sulik

*From pure spring water
in the golden pond of youth
Our mirrored reflections
smile back at us*

*We climb and rest
on top the highest ridge
Overlooking endless valleys
with meadows
Groves and channels
filled with sweet nectar
Surrounded by
humble creatures*

*The perfect orb
splashes sporadic streaks
Of orange
yellow and red
luminous light
On purple cottony clouds
in the powder blue sky
As it slips
into a deep pocket
Disappearing from view
to shine on the other side
of midnight*

*Twinkling stars
dot the vast universe
when I propose
Your smile glows
in the night
When you give me
your approval*

*Together we set
the world ablaze
Dancing the night away
in each other's arms
in harmony
Into the morning hours
when the sun returns*

Color of Laughter, Color of Tears

Oh, how I love
your tender touch
I believe
in the two of us
With love
our garden will grow
and thrive

Without you
I have no purpose
Oh, how I love you so.

— SRS —

Laurel A. Johnson/Stephen R. Sulik

Life's Toll

I no longer have soft skin for you to touch.
Life has taken its toll.
A rougher texture now replaces satin spaces,
velvet curves of youth where sparse lanugo
caught the candlelight
and trembled like antennae when you touched me.
Flaxen hair no longer gleams in sunlight,
with stray curly tendrils
you could wrap around your fingers
as a smile began to kindle in your eyes.
These days the scent that lingers there
is not the fresh-washed subtlety of younger days.
My chemistry has dissipated over time.
Watered down by circumstance and decades,
no longer fueled by estrogen and waxing moons,
still, it leads me on a merry chase.
I can't erase the memories of days when we were young.

I try to deny it, but life has taken its toll.

— LAJ —

Outcast

My thoughts return
from time to time
To my childhood years
when I was in grade school.

I remember standing outside
near two wooden doors
in back of the church
Watching my classmates
running and laughing
Up in the field
and on the playground
during our morning recess.

I didn't know at the time
during morning recess
Why I was drawn daily
like a magnet
To those two wooden
church doors
Until many years later.

From grade school
to high school
There were a couple
occasions
When I was invited
to my classmates
social events
But while there
I felt out of place.

I cried myself
to sleep at night
Often asking God
if there was something
wrong with me
But received
no answer
from Him
I soon began
to regret being born.

*High school graduation day
finally arrived and
there was a big celebration.
My classmates and I
had made it
But I still felt
as though I was not one
Of the group and
refrained from going
to the celebrations.*

*After graduation
my classmates and I
Went our separate ways
to learn about life.*

*It wasn't until
several years later
When I returned home
for a visit with Mom and Dad
That I learned something
about my classmates.*

*A few were happily married
and had children;
A few divorced;
A few became alcoholics;
A few became addicted to drugs.
A few were in jail and
A few dead.*

*On that same visit home
I walked
To the playground
where it all began
Twenty years earlier.*

*I stood once again
in the same spot-
Near the two
wooden church doors-
Alone with my thoughts
in the silent of night.*

Color of Laughter, Color of Tears

Standing in the dark
I soon realized
That God had
answered me
A long time ago.

I had decided
on my own
At a very early age
not to throw
the life
He had given me-
away.

I looked up
at the heavens
Smiled, laughed
and cried.
I had asked for guidance
from above
And received it
all during the years
Of growing into manhood.

Through those years
when I thought
I was alone
I didn't realize
He was there all along
watching over and carrying me
Until I was able
to find the courage
Within myself
to get off His back
and on my feet
To walk on my own
with Him again at my side.

I now cherish
those growing up years
It feels good
to be given the gift of life
Living it to its fullest
shedding no more tears
of regret.

Laurel A. Johnson/Stephen R. Sulik

I wrote this poem long ago
and did not know
That a few years after
writing it
When I was away
from home
I would lose my father
when he suffered
a heart attack
After attending Mass
one early spring morning
During the school's
morning recess
just a few feet inside
Those two wooden
church doors....
May peace be with you,
Dad
Thank you, too,
for those guidance years
You provided me
while I was growing up
- to be a man.

— SRS —

Markers

I didn't understand it then,
why she clutched that old cigar box
to her chest the way she did
and bit her lower lip to keep from crying.

I said, "What's wrong, Mom?"
as if a nine-year old could ease
or lend support to adult sorrow.

Piece by piece,
she laid each crumpled scrap of paper
on the table in our kitchen.
"Your father's markers."

Markers. What could they be
to make my mother cry?

That night, her tears shone golden
underneath the kitchen light.
I watched them fall,
wishing they would stop and she would smile
that sweet angelic smile of hers.
It always signaled all was well with us -
our family, her little brood.

Next to every marker signed by Dad's hand
she laid a fifty cent piece or two quarters
taken from my piggy bank
that grandparents or relatives kept fed
for future times. For clothes or treats.

She said, "I'm sorry, Honey. It has to be,"
then laid an envelope beside Dad's markers
and wrote a simple letter to accompany each one.

"I'll pay you something every week
until my husband's debt is cancelled.
It can't be much because I have four kids to feed.
I'll do my best.
Sincerely,
Verla Smith"

*I asked her why she had to pay my father's debts.
She said, "Because his debts are mine
and he's the father of my children."*

*Markers. Promises he made to bars
and gambling halls
where he charged drinks and poker losses
or danced with other women
while my mother waited crying in the dark.
I might have been a youngster,
but I knew the price my mother paid back then
and I've not forgotten now.*

*Golden was the color of her tears,
and silver were the coins she eked
to keep our father out of jail
and shame from her four children.*

— LAJ —

Worst Case Scenario

After less than one year of marriage
he broke her heart.
Although the doctor didn't say so at the time,
the damage was irreparable.
Her enthusiasm smothered out
because she couldn't breathe for days.
Joy died. She retreated
to a hidden corner of her mind.

In his defense he didn't understand.

Marriage in his family was business,
an association strictly for survival
and perpetuating children
Passion didn't enter into the equation
and his people couldn't comprehend
the concept of marital devotion
or the full meaning of emotion
based on dedication and single-minded trust.

When they met, her virginity
and inexperience along such lines
were paramount and necessary
if his life was to proceed along the path
it had when he was free.
He enjoyed the nightlife, wilder women,
and the leeway to pursue
if that desire should overtake him.

Well, he had his way,
but to his dying day he wished otherwise
With retrospective wisdom
he compared the past and present,
considered best and worst case scenarios,
wondering what might have been
between them from the start
if he had loved from the beginning.

—LAJ—

Benediction

For whatever remains of the natural world
in contrast to the shambles man has made of it,
I'm thankful for that blessing.

Because the awesome sky exists,
eyes can see beyond ghettoes and landfills
to catch at least a fleeting glimpse of wonder.

Flowers and forests, lightning and snow
cleanse our air of chemical impurities.
Is that not glorious to know?

Oceans wash forever to the shore
depositing man's cast off trash, and yet,
the deep supports a plethora of life.

Rocks reveal their history,
whether small enough to fit the palm
or towering majestically far distant.

Forever let me see and listen
beyond the ugly and mundane of life.
Let me find beauty everywhere I turn.

—LAJ —

Untitled Poem

Then the gods spoke
unto the people;
We made it a Creed
for all of you
And for all times
to come;
We say unto you
that on this earth
All men who tremble –
shall live afraid;
All men who battle –
shall die in battle
And only those who
Love –
Shall reap of this life and
Plant the seeds
for tomorrow.

You cannot change the future – unless you know the lessons –
of the past.
Love is the one thing – that kills an angry man.

Author Unknown
Greek Civilization
2nd Century B.C.

About the Authors

Stephen R. Sulik has been in law enforcement for thirty years and recently retired from the Pasadena Texas Police Department. He is now employed by another Texas police agency. His first book of poetry, **In Search of Nature's Hidden Secrets,** was published in 1982 in Houston Texas. It is no longer in print, but selections from that book do appear in **Color of Laughter, Color of Tears.** Stephen has authored two books of fiction – **Random Ransom**, published in 1991, *no longer in print,* and **The Tattered Coat,** released by PublishAmerica in 2002. Future books in the series are now in the planning stages.

Laurel Johnson is a somewhat reclusive author living in the rural reaches of Nebraska with her husband of several decades and their cats. Her book of poetry and prose – **The Grass Dance** – was released by PublishAmerica in 2001. A work of fiction – **The Alley of Wishes** - was released as a second edition in August 2003 by Dandelion Books of Tempe AZ. She is a senior reviewer for *Midwest Book Review;* submitting staff member to *Quill Quarterly Poetry Review* and *The Pedestal Magazine;* and Review Editor for *New Works Review.* She is currently working on several books.

Printed in the United States
35604LVS00005B/81